CONTENTS

<u>CHAPTER 0</u>

Preamble

A difficult lesson about history is that it appears to repeat itself.

History repeats itself.

History repeats itself.

CHAPTER 1

Economics

History repeats itself.

History repeats itself.

History repeats itself.

History repeats itself.

History repeats itself.

History repeats itself.

History repeats itself.

History repeats itself.

History repeats itself.

History repeats itself.

History repeats itself.

History repeats itself.

History repeats itself.

CHAPTER 2

Education

History repeats itself.

History repeats itself.

History repeats itself.

History repeats itself.

History repeats itself.

History repeats itself.

History repeats itself.

History repeats itself.

History repeats itself.

History repeats itself.

History repeats itself.

History repeats itself.

History repeats itself.

History repeats itself.

History repeats itself.

CHAPTER 3

Civil Rights

History repeats itself.

History repeats itself.

History repeats itself.

History repeats itself.

History repeats itself.

History repeats itself.

History repeats itself.

History repeats itself.

History repeats itself.

History repeats itself.

History repeats itself.

History repeats itself.

History repeats itself.

CHAPTER 4

Crime

History repeats itself.

History repeats itself.

History repeats itself.

History repeats itself.

History repeats itself.

History repeats itself.

History repeats itself.

History repeats itself.

History repeats itself.

History repeats itself.

History repeats itself.

History repeats itself.

History repeats itself.

CHAPTER 5

Energy

History repeats itself.

History repeats itself.

History repeats itself.

History repeats itself.

History repeats itself.

History repeats itself.

History repeats itself.

History repeats itself.

History repeats itself.

History repeats itself.

History repeats itself.

History repeats itself.

History repeats itself.

History repeats itself.

History repeats itself.

History repeats itself.

History repeats itself.

History repeats itself.

History repeats itself.

History repeats itself.

History repeats itself.

History repeats itself.

History repeats itself.

History repeats itself.

History repeats itself.

History repeats itself.

History repeats itself.

CHAPTER 6

Foreign Policy

History repeats itself.

History repeats itself.

History repeats itself.

History repeats itself.

History repeats itself.

History repeats itself.

History repeats itself.

History repeats itself.

History repeats itself.

History repeats itself.

History repeats itself.

History repeats itself.

History repeats itself.

History repeats itself.

History repeats itself.

History repeats itself.

History repeats itself.

History repeats itself.

History repeats itself.

History repeats itself.

History repeats itself.

History repeats itself.

History repeats itself.

History repeats itself.

History repeats itself.

History repeats itself.

History repeats itself.

CHAPTER 7

Immigration

History repeats itself.

History repeats itself.

History repeats itself.

History repeats itself.

History repeats itself.

History repeats itself.

History repeats itself.

History repeats itself.

History repeats itself.

History repeats itself.

History repeats itself.

History repeats itself.

History repeats itself.

History repeats itself.

History repeats itself.

History repeats itself.

History repeats itself.

History repeats itself.

History repeats itself.

History repeats itself.

History repeats itself.

History repeats itself.

History repeats itself.

History repeats itself.

History repeats itself.

History repeats itself.

History repeats itself.

History repeats itself.

History repeats itself.

History repeats itself.

History repeats itself.

History repeats itself.

History repeats itself.

CHAPTER 8

National Security

History repeats itself.

History repeats itself.

History repeats itself.

History repeats itself.

History repeats itself.

History repeats itself.

History repeats itself.

History repeats itself.

History repeats itself.

History repeats itself.

History repeats itself.

History repeats itself.

History repeats itself.

History repeats itself.

History repeats itself.

History repeats itself.

History repeats itself.

History repeats itself.

History repeats itself.

History repeats itself.

History repeats itself.

History repeats itself.

History repeats itself.

History repeats itself.

History repeats itself.

History repeats itself.

History repeats itself.

History repeats itself.

History repeats itself.

CHAPTER 9

Principles

History repeats itself.

History repeats itself.

History repeats itself.

History repeats itself.

History repeats itself.

History repeats itself.

History repeats itself.

History repeats itself.

History repeats itself.

History repeats itself.

History repeats itself.

History repeats itself.

History repeats itself.

History repeats itself.

History repeats itself.

History repeats itself.

History repeats itself.

History repeats itself.

History repeats itself.

History repeats itself.

History repeats itself.

History repeats itself.

History repeats itself.

History repeats itself.

History repeats itself.

A difficult lesson about history is that history repeats itself.